MENTORING SCHOOL PRINCIPALS: 200 LESSONS FOR LEADERSHIP SUCCESS

DR DHEERAJ MEHROTRA ZEBA PARVEEN

Contents

Preface

Mentoring School Principals: 200 Lessons for Leadership Success has expanded to 198 lessons to reflect school leadership's large, dynamic landscape. When we started writing this, we envisioned a mentor's voice in 200 bites of wisdom. The principalship is not a modest calling. It's a big, chaotic, magnificent calling that requires more than a few lessons. So here we are with 200—not exhaustive, but a fuller route map. This book isn't ivory tower theory. It comes from decades of witnessing principals rise, falter, and soar—mine and others. We've sat in tense staff rooms, cheered at unlikely substitutions and proxies, and supported leaders through days they wanted to resign. These are the hard-won facts of those moments, formed as if we were across the table from you with coffee, saying, "Here's what I've learnt. Try this."

The teachings are from laying foundations to engaging families and are critical for any new principal. It follows the advanced talents, innovate boldly, bond communities, face crises, and evolve as a person, not simply a leader. They form a toolkit—pick one a day, dwell on a couple, or share with your team. You can use them.

Principalship is like commanding an orchestra while tuning mid-song. You're a visionary, fixer, and cheerleader while the music plays. It's exhausting, thrilling, and irreplaceable. These pages should be like a mentor, pushing you ahead, reminding you to breathe, and celebrating your little victories.

School Leadership doesn't require perfection. It requires grit, heart, and a growth mindset. While your school's issues are unique, these lessons will help you see through the fog. There's something for everyone, from beginners to veterans reconsidering their legacy. Turn the page. Jump in anywhere. Principalship is a journey with others. Let's work—and maybe enjoy it.

- Authors

CHAPTER ONE

A NOTE TO THE MENTORS!

Effective leadership is no longer sufficient to be concerned with preserving order or simply fulfilling benchmarks; instead, it is also concerned with encouraging innovation, cultivating resilience, and guiding institutions through challenging situations. The acquisition of these abilities is of the utmost importance since they directly influence the outcomes for students, the morale of staff members, and the overall health of a school community.

Incorporating technology into educational settings, such as artificial intelligence (AI) programs like PowerSchool or Century Tech, is one of the most compelling reasons for this necessity. These technologies must not only be understood by school administrators, but they must also be used to strategically guide the adoption of these tools. This will ensure that the tools improve learning without overwhelming staff or worsening equity disparities. A combination of technical literacy and visionary thinking is required for this, as they are the qualities that enable leaders to establish alignment between digital change and educational objectives. As an illustration, a principal proficient in data analytics might use the insights provided by systems such as BrightBytes to identify pupils who are having difficulty early on, effectively directing resources.

The capacity to manage a wide variety of stakeholders is also essential. Pupils in today's schools come from a wide range of cultural, socioeconomic, and linguistic backgrounds, and each has their specific requirements. Leaders must develop their emotional intelligence and cultural competency to create welcoming workplaces and ensure that every voice is heard. Every day, this ability is tested, whether it is addressing concerns raised by parents, providing support to teachers under pressure, or campaigning for funds. The school's foundation can be strengthened by a head who excels in this area since they can transform possible conflicts into chances for collaboration.

Additionally, the post-pandemic environment has increased the demand for flexible leadership. Because of the learning gaps and the mental health issues that students and staff are experiencing, heads must strike a balance between empathy and decisiveness. Leaders can stabilise their schools while also moving forward if they have mastered crisis management and change leadership skills, similar to the concentration on results in emergencies that the coercive style emphasises. As an illustration, a principal would implement a new attendance policy to combat chronic absenteeism. This would include using clear communication and data to garner support, demonstrating authority and commitment.

Another area in which leadership abilities are non-negotiable is the responsibility of staff development. Teachers struggle with burnout and excessive expectations, and there is also a rising concern about retaining talent. It is possible for leaders who are skilled in coaching, mentoring, and professional development to empower their colleagues, thereby cultivating a culture that emphasises growth rather than tiredness. This can be accomplished by employing training tools like Disco AI. Not only does this improve morale, but it also improves the quality of instruction, which directly benefits the pupils.

Last but not least, the pressure to achieve quantitative outcomes, including testing scores, graduation rates, and college placements, continues to be unrelenting. Leaders who master strategic planning and accountability can create lofty but still attainable goals. This allows them to align resources and efforts across the entire school. This ability is similar to the coercive leadership quality of demanding excellence; however, it flourishes most effectively when combined with inspiration rather than just enforcement.

Acquiring the abilities necessary for school leadership is essential to achieve success in education in 2025 and after. Blending vision with execution, empathy with determination, and innovation with tradition are all critical components in this process. Heads who can respond to this challenge do more than manage schools; they transform them by catering to the requirements of the present while also planning for the unpredictability of the future. The futures of the students, the community's trust, and the institution's heritage are all too important to settle for anything less.

CHAPTER TWO

Mastering School Leadership Skills

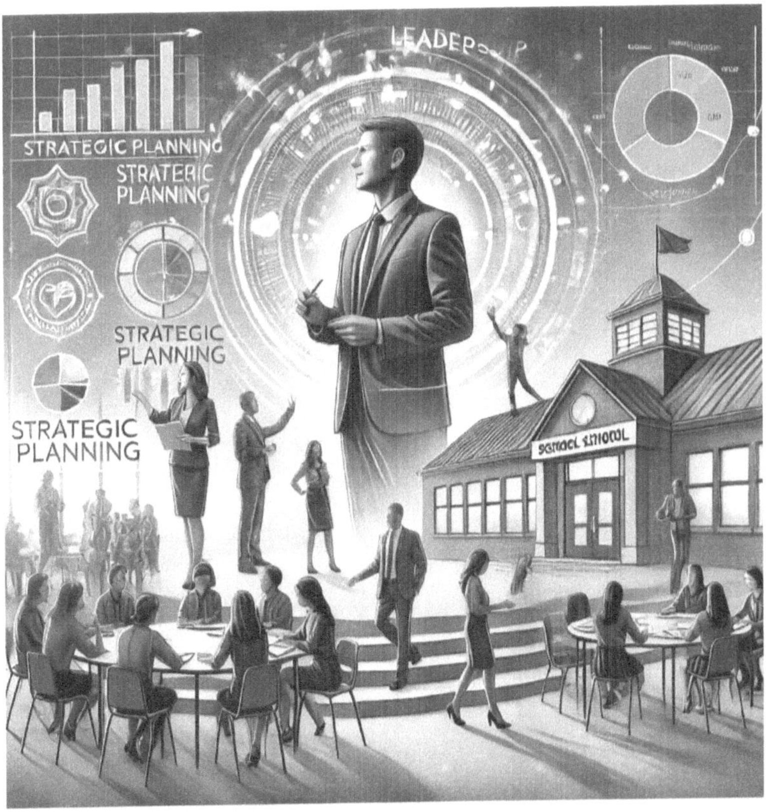

Effective school leadership is not about power—it's about empowering others to reach their full potential.

Clarify your leadership purpose to motivate those around you.

Learn your school's unique history to inform its direction.

Create a distinct vision to steer your school forward.

Stay present by engaging with the school community daily.

Prioritize listening to uncover valuable insights.

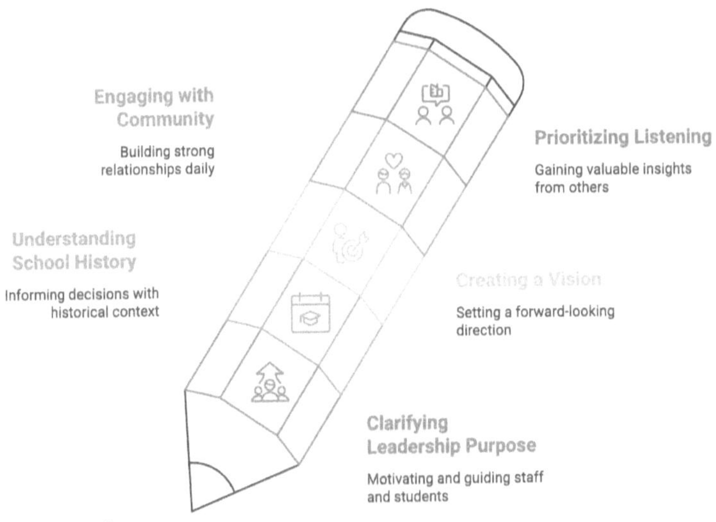

Remain composed during stressful situations.

Acknowledge errors to strengthen trust with your team.

Assign tasks effectively to encourage staff ownership.

Guard your schedule to focus on what matters most.

Adjust to change with flexibility and grace.

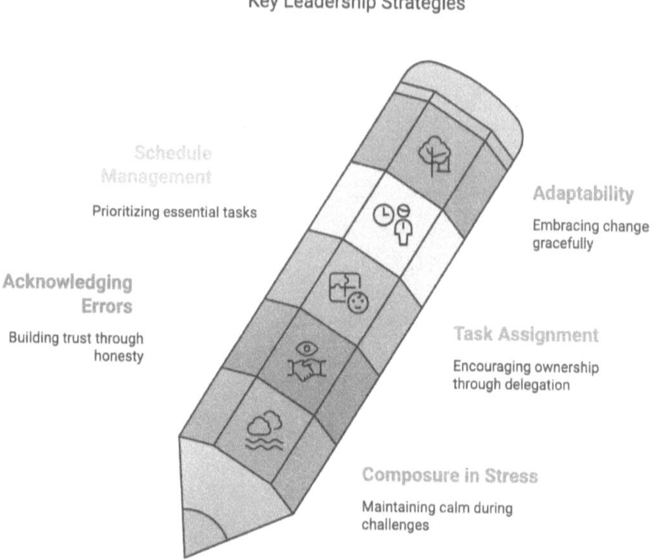

Cultivate toughness to handle adversity well.

Accept your boundaries as a human leader.

Invite critiques to refine your approach.

Highlight minor victories to boost morale.

Keep questioning to maintain a learner's mindset.

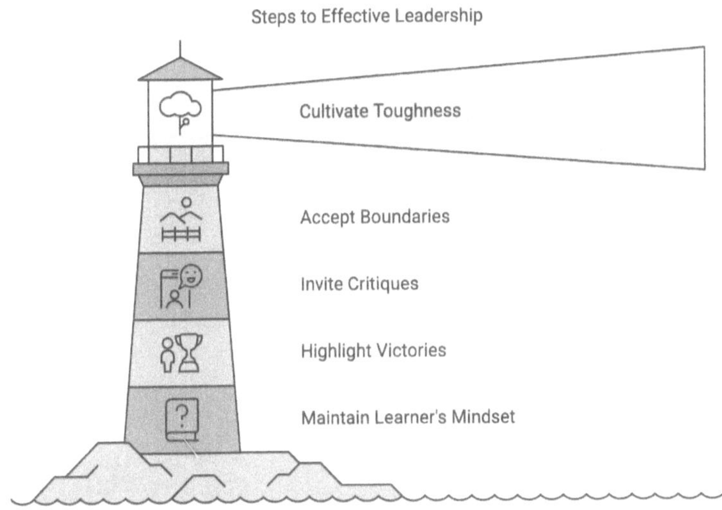

Demonstrate what you expect from others through actions.

Rely on instincts alongside factual analysis.

Act with honour to establish a lasting reputation.

Pursue constant growth to avoid stagnation.

Welcome interaction by being accessible to all.

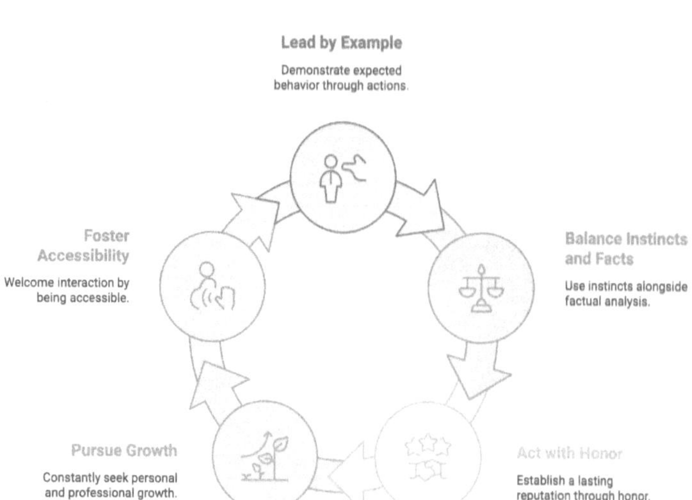

Focus on culture first, valuing people over plans.

Project positivity to influence the school's vibe.

Preserve meaningful customs while introducing fresh ideas.

Earn trust through strong relationships.

Include everyone's input—staff, students, and beyond.

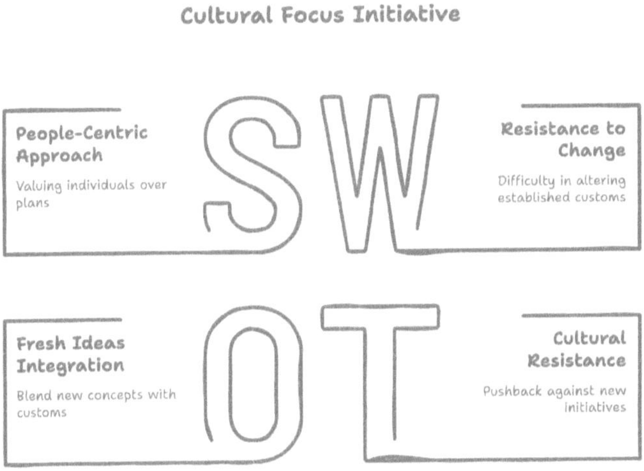

Cultural Focus Initiative

Settle disputes swiftly to prevent escalation.

Unite your team to break down barriers.

Appreciate hard work to keep motivation high.

Show hopefulness to spread encouragement.

Establish routines that bring people together.

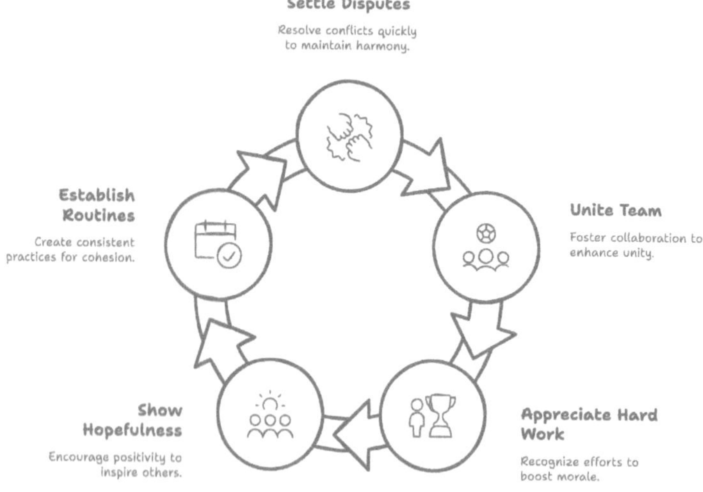

Confront pessimism before it spreads.

Support bold moves to foster development.

Embrace differences to enrich the school.

Maintain steadiness for a secure environment.

Speak plainly to avoid mix-ups.

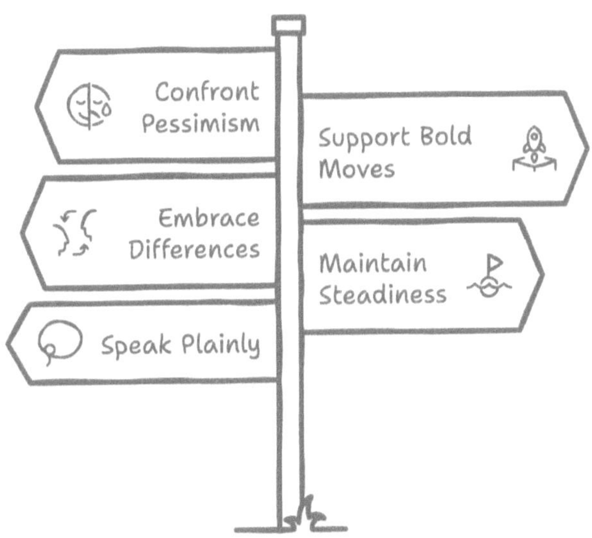

Promote well-being to keep staff thriving.

Instill school spirit by showcasing successes.

14

Lighten the mood with shared laughter.

Remember names to forge personal ties.

Stay modest to connect authentically.

Staff Well-being

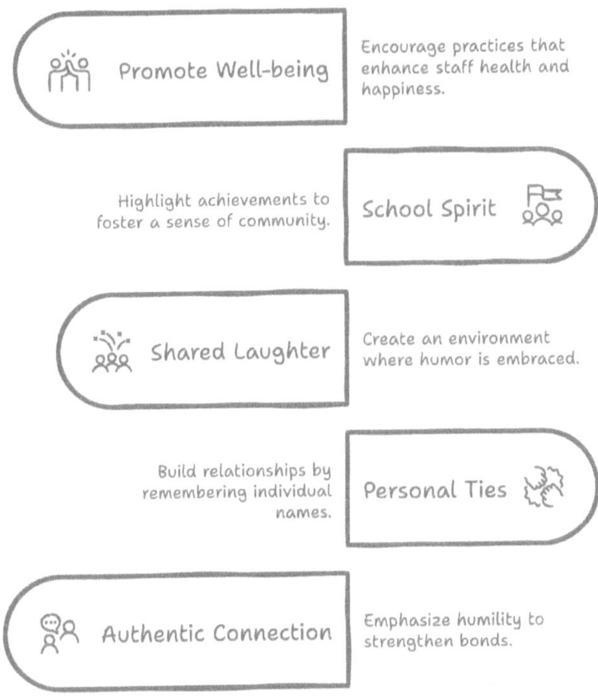

Strengthen your staff by empowering them.

Recruit for alignment, prioritizing character over skills.

Guide without controlling to build confidence.

Allow teaching freedom within a supportive framework.

Invest in development as a necessity, not a luxury.

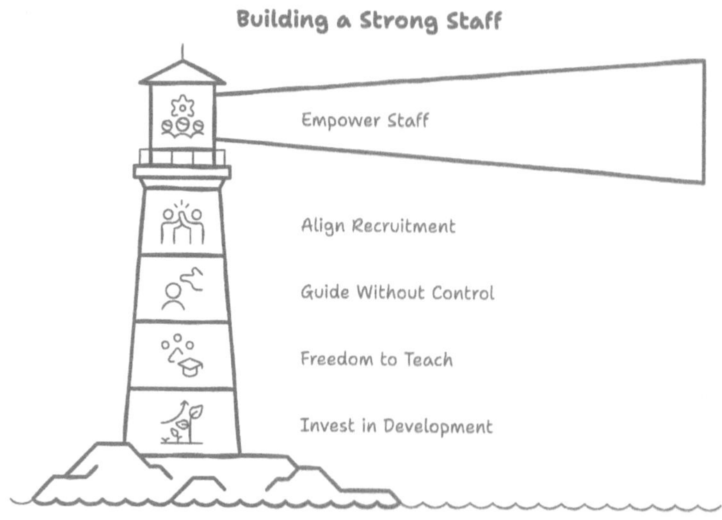

Hear concerns to find hidden fixes.

Shield staff time from pointless interruptions.

Spot potential in overlooked team members.

Provide growth-focused feedback, not fault-finding.

Give credit to teachers for their wins.

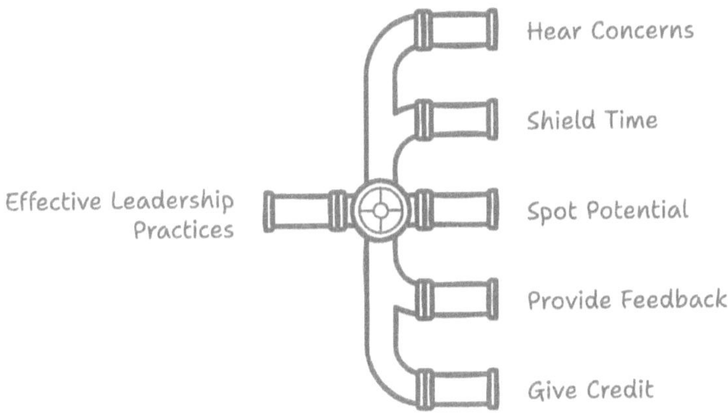

Stand by your team in challenging times.

Link personal goals to the school's mission.

Show appreciation often and sincerely.

Tackle exhaustion before it takes hold.

Streamline tasks to reduce frustration.

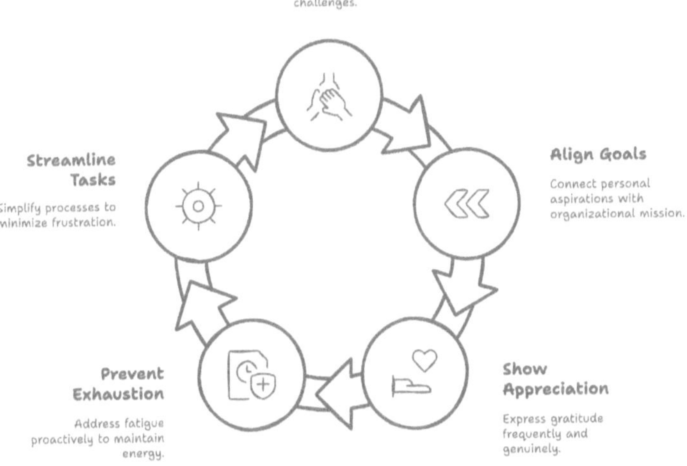

Welcome new approaches to teaching.

Champion staff needs to be decision-makers.

Honour personal time for a balanced team.

Nurture leadership in every teacher.

Rejoice in teamwork wins to solidify bonds.

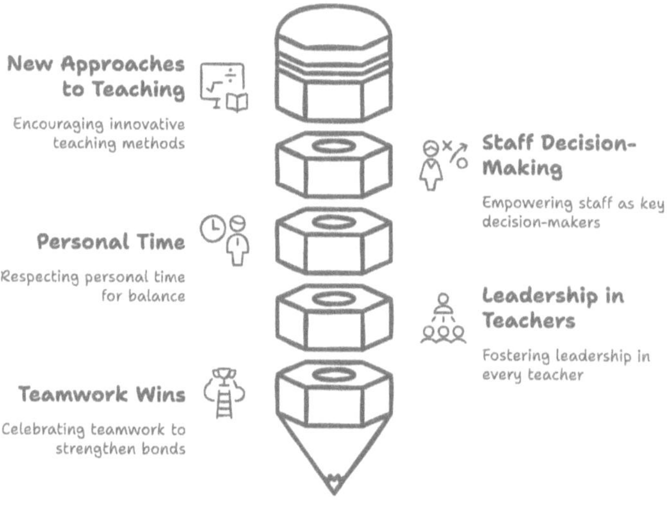

Connect with students by learning who they are.

Support their passions by attending their activities.

Correct with compassion, aiming to educate.

Engage families early to form alliances.

Keep parents updated with regular outreach.

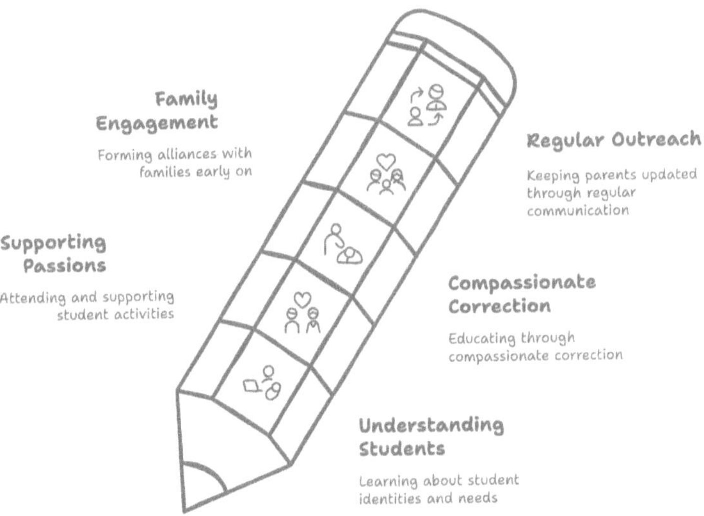

Encourage family insights to improve the school.

Dispel rumours with clear facts.

Publicly honour students for their efforts.

Respond to student struggles with understanding.

Raise the bar for every learner.

Infuse joy into the school experience.

Enforce rules kindly but firmly.

Grasp community dynamics to serve it better.

Organize gatherings to deepen ties.

Aid all students somewhat, especially those in need.

Teach practical skills beyond academics.

Greet kids daily to build rapport.

Stay cool in emergencies to reassure others.

Create lasting traditions for school unity.

Value student culture by staying in tune.

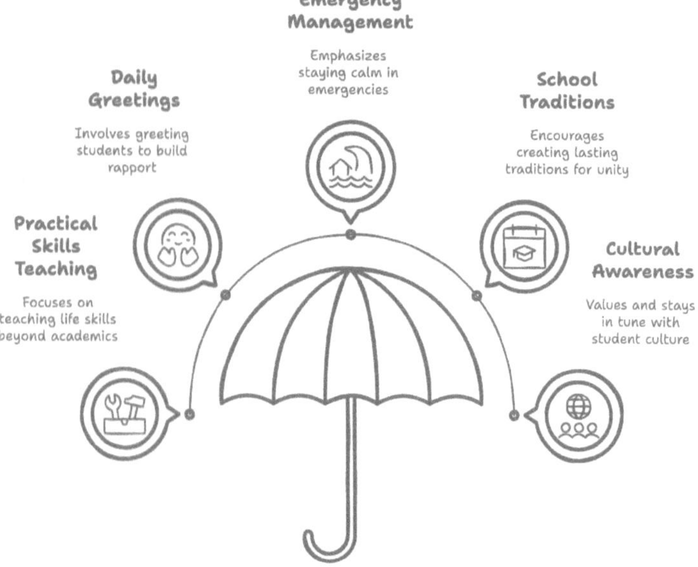

Prepare proactively for potential issues.

Lead change gently, not by mandate.

Oversee funds wisely to maximize impact.

Know regulations to stay compliant.

Find a middle ground in tough negotiations.

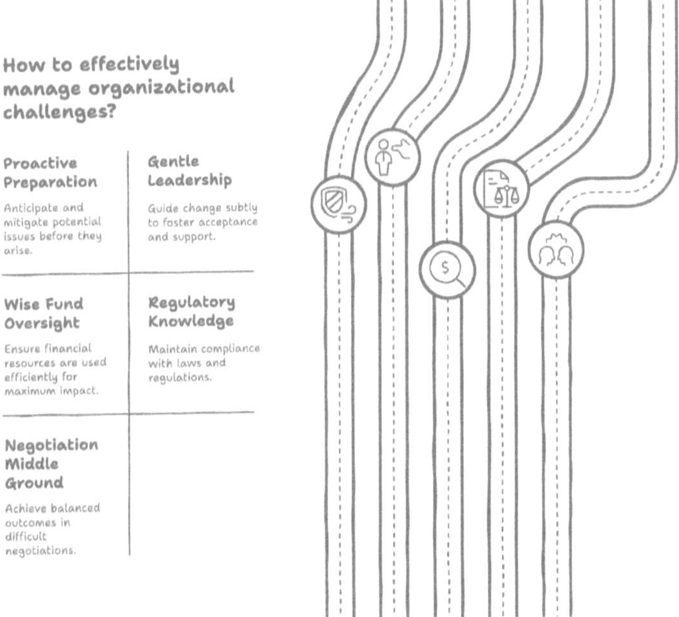

Endure critique with strength and openness.

Harmonize priorities among diverse groups.

Keep up with tech to enhance learning.

Link with peers for shared wisdom.

Regularly review and tweak strategies.

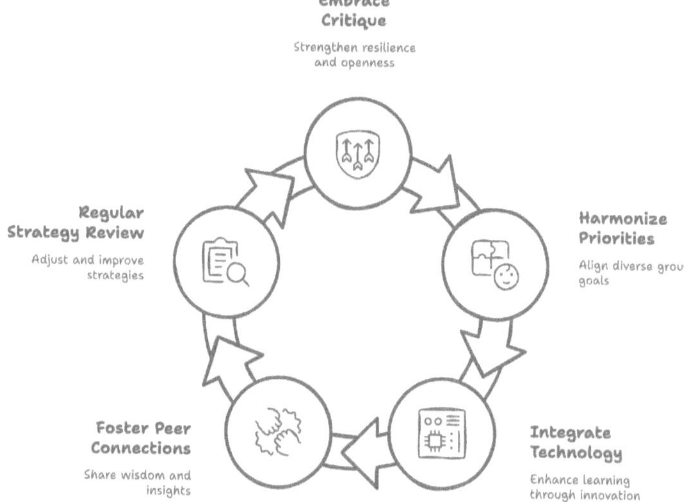

Rest intentionally to sustain energy.

Find advisors with seasoned perspectives.

Learn from setbacks rather than fear them.

Track education trends to stay relevant.

Push for resources your school requires.

Gauge progress with data and anecdotes.

Never stop learning as a leader.

Prepare a handover for smooth transitions.

Cherish your role to fuel dedication.

Plan for the future in every choice you make.

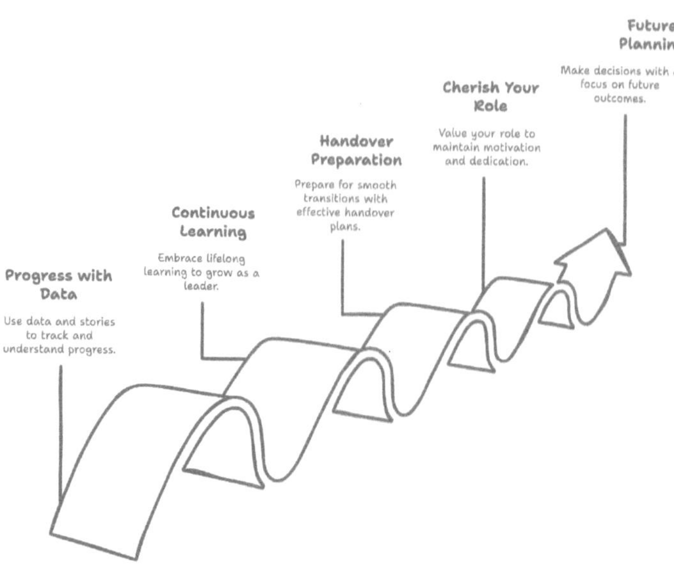

Handle tricky chats with honesty and care.

Gather allies to bolster your efforts.

Decide firmly to maintain trust.

Sense the mood to lead effectively.

Shape the story of your school's journey.

Question old ways when they no longer work.

Act amid uncertainty with confidence.

Anticipate shifts in education's landscape.

Blend ambition with precision in execution.

Ignite faith in your team's capabilities.

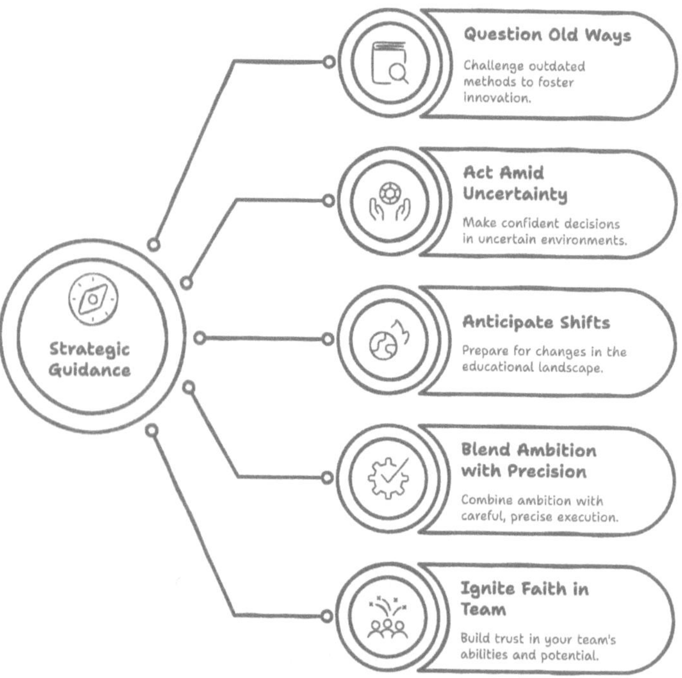

Remove excess to sharpen focus.

Think strategically in all you do.

Play to the strengths of your team.

Wield influence for reason, not control.

Grow successors to ensure continuity.

Leadership Principles Cycle

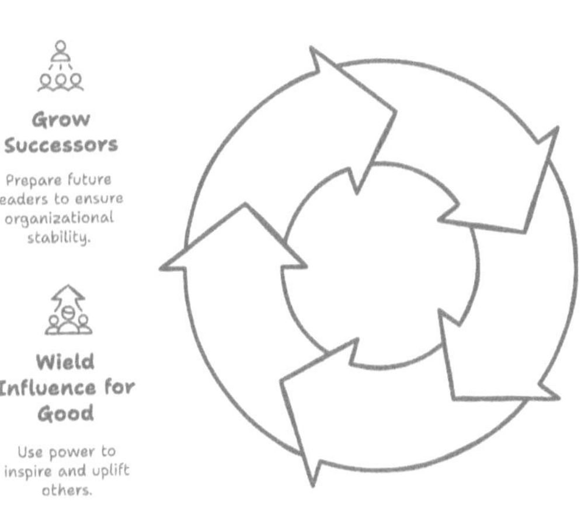

Stay humble amid achievements.

Test limits to drive progress.

Pause thoughtfully to enhance dialogue.

Persist relentlessly through obstacles.

Try new concepts on a small scale first.

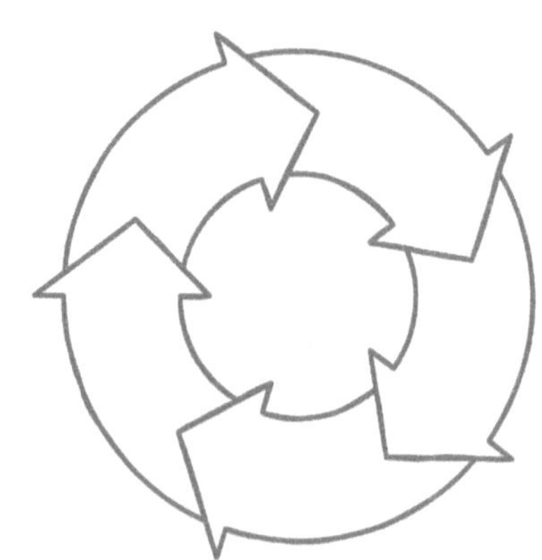

Adopt technology to enrich education.

Revamp timetables to suit learning needs.

Allow trial and error for breakthroughs.

Lead proactively to stay cutting-edge.

Mix heritage with novelty for balance.

Ask students what inspires them.

Refresh spaces to spark engagement.

Champion the arts as vital learning.

Make learning playful to hook interest.

Collaborate with specialists for fresh ideas.

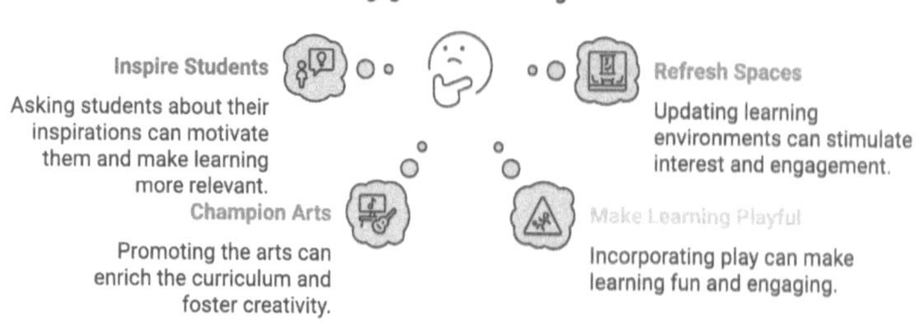

Reassess benchmarks for actual value.

Focus on solutions in teaching.

Harness data to guide choices.

Design adaptability into operations.

Boost STEM focus for future readiness.

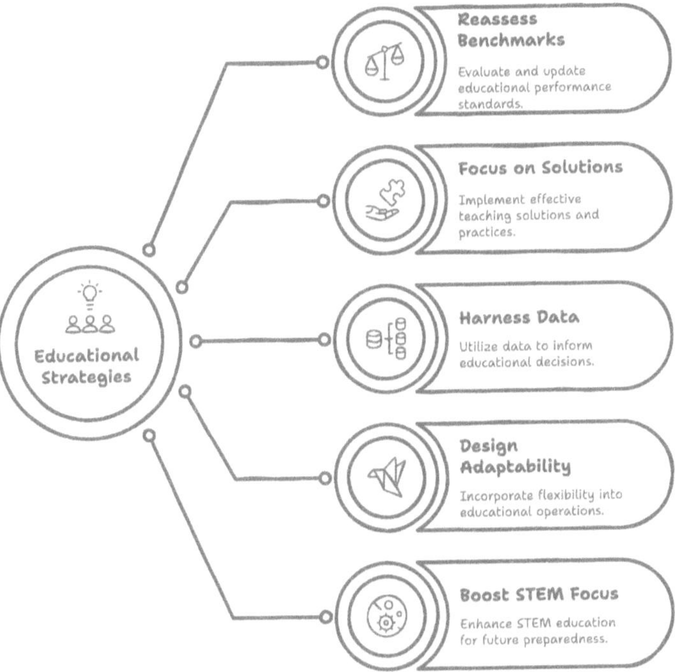

Weave in emotional learning for resilience.

Rethink assignments for real impact.

Adopt eco-friendly practices to teach care.

Broaden horizons with a global lens.

Understand your area to meet its demands.

Invite the community for shared events.

Work with local firms for mutual gain.

Involve past students for legacy support.

Hold open talks for community voices.

Broadcast achievements to build pride.

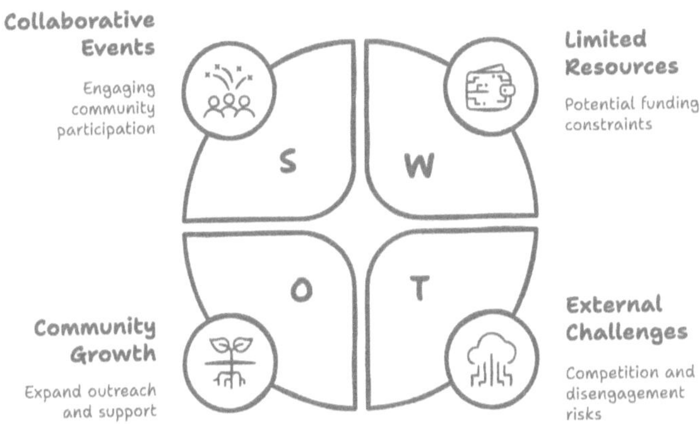

Back local efforts to earn goodwill.

Heal community rifts for unity.

Use the press to elevate your school's image.

Navigate politics while holding values.

Craft an identity that stands out.

Honour local diversity in celebrations.

Tackle hardship to support students.

Engage helpers to lighten the load.

Correct false views with positive proof.

Strategize outreach for lasting ties.

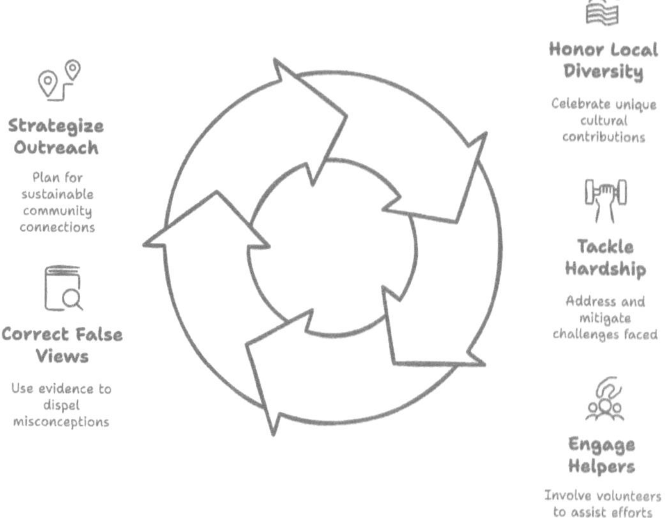

Model civic duty for students to follow.

Be open to maintaining trust.

Respect experience from community seniors.

Link people for a stronger whole.

Be ready for emergencies with thorough plans.

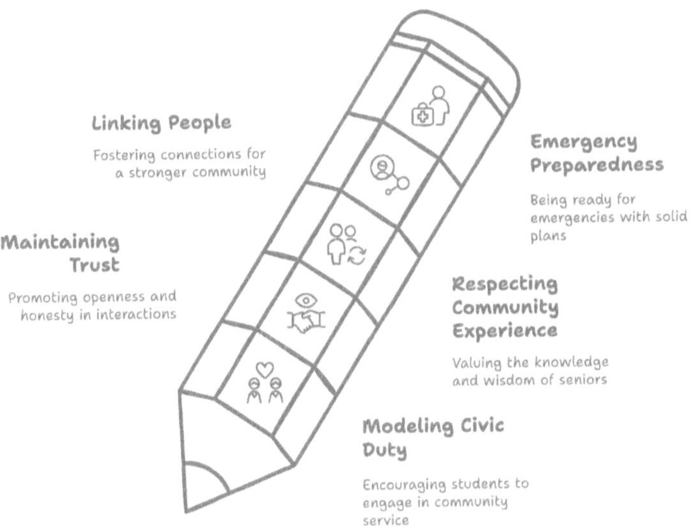

Share updates fast when crises hit.

Offer comfort during hard times.

Calm tensions with steady words.

Know key contacts for quick action.

Analyze mishaps to improve next time.

42

Effective Communication Strategies in Crisis Management

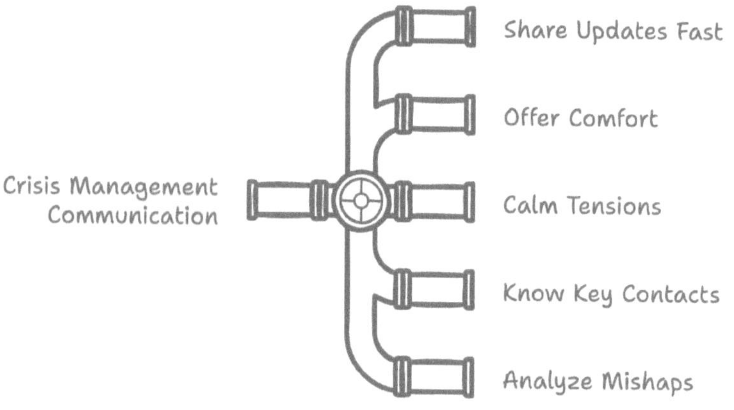

Defend your crew from undue criticism.

Speak to the media with poise and truth.

Bridge disagreements through discussion.

Remain impartial in disputes.

Map recovery after disruptions.

How to handle crew and media interactions?

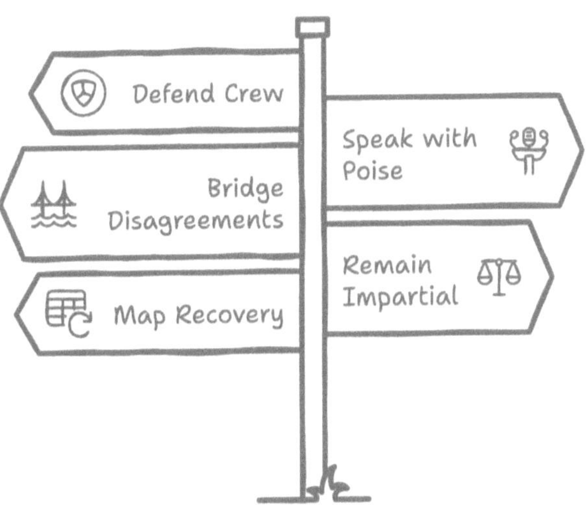

Equip staff for safety awareness.

Act firmly against harassment.

Counter rumours with reality.

Hold firm when chaos strikes.

Follow legal guidelines in conflicts.

Aid those hurt with resources and time.

Record details for clarity later.

Get advice in turbulent moments.

Recover strongly to lead forward.

Rekindle your drive to stay energized.

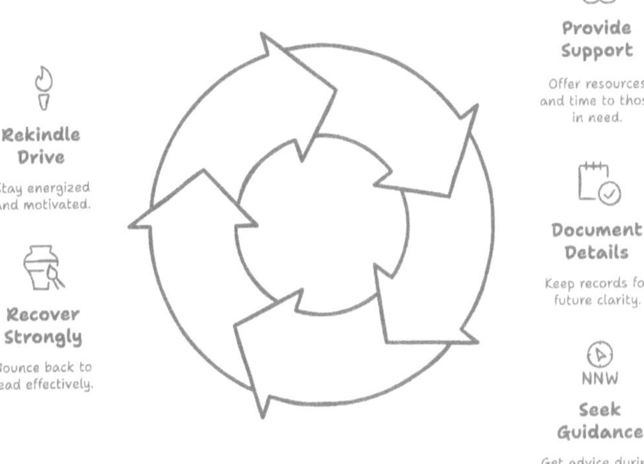

Set limits to protect your well-being.

Explore diverse reading for inspiration.

Stay active to keep sharp.

Find calm through quiet reflection.

Laugh easily to reduce strain.

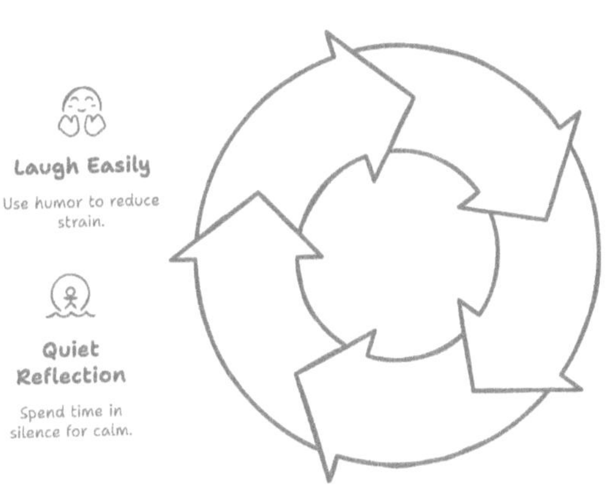

Keep friendships outside of work.

Enjoy pursuits that recharge you.

Look back weekly to adjust your path.

Guide others to enhance your growth.

Decline overload to stay focused.

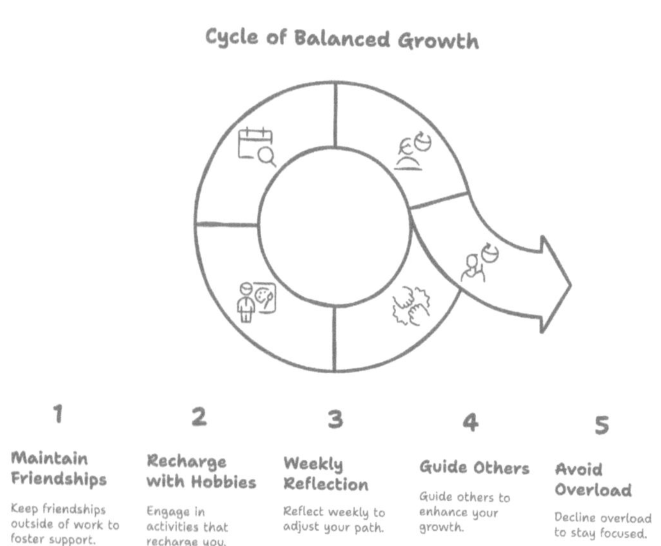

Mark successes with your team.

Practice gratitude for perspective.

Exit gracefully when the time comes.

Note your journey for future lessons.

Let go of guilt over past errors.

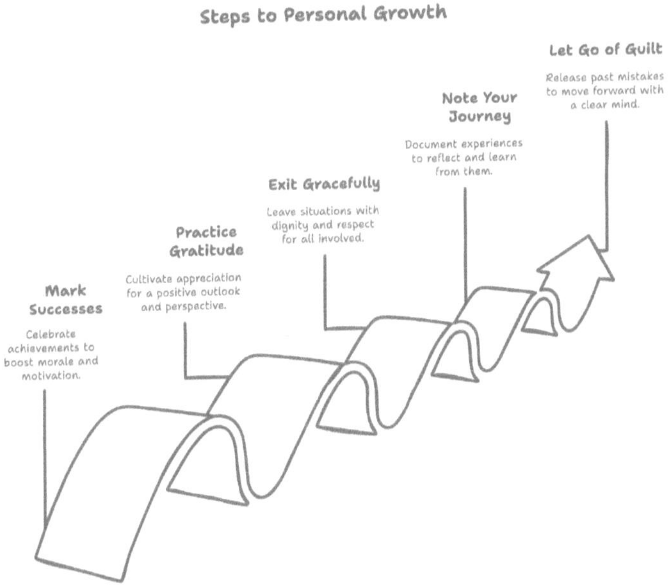

Motivate students to aim high.

Shape your impact through daily work.

Evolve continually as a leader.

Analyze trends to refine your strategies.

Invest smartly in learning priorities.

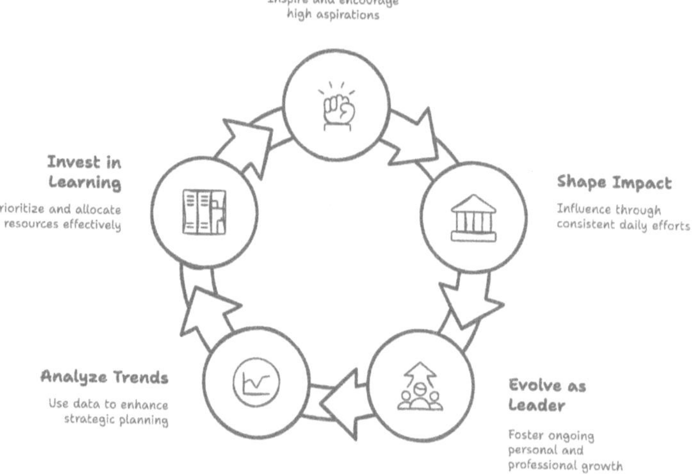

51

CHAPTER THREE

LEADERSHIP SCENARIOS

The best principals don't just manage schools; they create an environment where learning and leadership flourish together.

Case Study 1: Managing Teacher Burnout

Scenario:

Principal Abhishek Gautam of Royal High School noticed a decline in teacher morale halfway through the school year. Attendance at staff meetings is low, and several veteran teachers have submitted complaints about overwhelming workloads due to new district mandates requiring additional data tracking. Standardized test scores are slipping, and parents are beginning to voice concerns. Abhishek must decide how to address the issue without alienating her staff or the district leadership.

Advice Given:

Abhishek consults her Vice Principal, Reema Shah, who suggests conducting an anonymous staff survey to pinpoint specific pain points. She advises using the results to propose a streamlined version of the data-tracking requirements to the area while organizing a voluntary professional development day focused on stress management and work-life balance, funded through a small grant. Additionally, the school counsellor, Smita Gupta, recommends creating a peer support program where teachers can share strategies for managing workload.

Decision Point:

Smita must decide whether to implement these suggestions, oppose the district entirely, or maintain the status quo to avoid conflict. What are the potential risks and benefits of each option?

Suggested Strategies

1. Conducting an Anonymous Staff Survey

Advice from Vice Principal Reema Shah:

Reema suggests conducting an anonymous staff survey to identify specific pain points among teachers. This approach allows staff to voice their concerns without fear of repercussions, providing valuable insights into the underlying issues affecting morale.

Benefits:

Gathers direct feedback from teachers, fostering a sense of involvement.

Identify specific areas of concern that can be addressed.

Helps build trust between administration and staff.

Risks:

Potentially negative feedback may lead to further dissatisfaction if not appropriately handled.

Time and resources needed to analyze survey results.

2. Proposing a Streamlined Version of Data-Tracking Requirements

Advice from Reema:

Reema recommends proposing a streamlined version of the data-tracking requirements to the district using the survey results. This could alleviate some of the burdens on teachers while still meeting district expectations.

Benefits:

Reduces workload for teachers, potentially improving morale.

Show district leadership that the school is proactive in addressing concerns.

Maintains compliance with district mandates.

Risks:

The district may reject the proposal, leading to frustration among staff.

Risk of appearing non-compliant if the proposal is not accepted.

3. Organizing a Voluntary Professional Development Day

Advice from Reema:

Reema also suggests organizing a voluntary professional development day funded by a small grant focusing on stress management and work-life balance.

Benefits:

Provides teachers with tools to manage stress and workload.

Encourages a culture of self-care and support among staff.

Can improve overall morale and job satisfaction.

Risks:

Low attendance may indicate a lack of interest or further disengagement.

Requires careful planning and execution to be effective.

4. Creating a Peer Support Program

Advice from School Counsellor Smita Gupta:

Smita recommends establishing a peer support program where teachers can share strategies for managing their workload and stress.

Benefits:

Fosters collaboration and camaraderie among staff.

Provides a platform for sharing best practices and resources.

Can lead to innovative solutions to common challenges.

Risks:

May require additional time commitment from teachers.

Effectiveness depends on participation and engagement.

Decision Point

Principal Abhishek Gautam must weigh the options of implementing the suggested strategies, opposing the district mandates, or maintaining the status quo.

Option Analysis

Implement Suggestions:

Benefits: Addresses teacher concerns, improves morale, and fosters a supportive environment.

Risks: Potential pushback from the district and the need to carefully manage staff expectations.

Oppose the District:

Benefits: Could lead to immediate relief for teachers and a strong stance on their behalf.

Risks: May alienate district leadership, jeopardizing future support and resources.

Maintain Status Quo:

Benefits: Avoids conflict and maintains current operations.

Risks: Continued decline in morale and performance, leading to long-term negative consequences for the school.

Conclusion

Principal Abhishek Gautam faces a critical decision that will impact the morale of her staff and the overall performance of Royal High School. By carefully considering the advice from her Vice Principal and School Counsellor and weighing the potential risks and benefits of each option, Abhishek can take meaningful steps toward improving the situation while maintaining a positive relationship with both her staff and district leadership.

Case Study 2: Addressing Bullying in the Digital Age

Scenario:

Concerned parents alerted Padam Public School Principal Jyoti Gupta about anonymous social media posts targeting several students. The posts include humiliating, photoshopped images and threatening messages. The incidents appear to originate off-campus but affect student attendance and classroom dynamics. The school's anti-bullying policy is outdated and doesn't explicitly cover cyberbullying.

Advice Given:

The school's IT specialist, Rohan Sharma, advises Jyoti to collaborate with local law enforcement to trace the accounts and identify the perpetrators, emphasizing that this could deter further incidents. Meanwhile, the school's guidance counsellor, Deepa David, suggests hosting a series of assemblies on digital citizenship for students and parents, paired with a revision of the bullying policy to include online behaviour. A veteran teacher, Mrs Heema Joshi, cautions against a heavy-handed approach, recommending restorative justice circles to address the root causes without escalating tensions.

Decision Point:

Jyoti must weigh whether to pursue a punitive response, focus on education and policy reform, or attempt a restorative approach. How should she balance student safety with community trust?

Decision & Justification for Addressing Cyberbullying

After carefully considering the concerns of parents, school staff, and students, Principal Jyoti Gupta decides on a three-pronged approach that balances immediate action, education, and long-term policy reform:

1?? Immediate Action: Identifying the Source & Ensuring Safety

IT Specialist Rohan Sharma advised that we should collaborate with local law enforcement to trace the anonymous accounts and deter future incidents.

Ensure affected students feel safe by providing counseling support and increased monitoring of social dynamics.

Justification: Student safety is the top priority. Identifying the perpetrators ensures accountability and sends a strong message against cyberbullying while preventing further harm.

2?? Educational Initiative: Digital Citizenship Awareness

The IT department and guidance counselor, Deepa David, organised assemblies and workshops for students and parents.

Focus on responsible online behavior, the consequences of cyberbullying, and digital empathy.

Justification: Punitive measures alone won't prevent future incidents. Teaching students about responsible digital behavior builds a culture of respect and accountability.

3?? Policy Reform & Restorative Justice

Revise the school's anti-bullying policy to include cyberbullying explicitly and outline clear consequences.

Implement restorative justice circles, as suggested by Mrs. Heema Joshi, allowing students to discuss the impact of cyberbullying and resolve conflicts constructively.

Justification: An updated policy ensures long-term protection, while restorative practices help address underlying issues and encourage responsible behavior without alienating students.

Message to Stakeholders:

? To Parents: "We are taking immediate action to ensure student safety while fostering a culture of responsible online behavior."
? To Students: "Cyberbullying has serious consequences, but our goal is also to educate and empower you to use social media responsibly."
? To Teachers & Staff: "Updating our policies and engaging students in restorative dialogue will help prevent future incidents while maintaining a positive school climate."

This approach ensures swift action against perpetrators, educational growth for the school community, and long-term policy improvements—creating a safer, more responsible digital environment for all. ?

#CyberbullyingPrevention
#StudentSafety
#EducationMatters

#DigitalCitizenship
#SchoolLeadership

Case Study 3: Allocating a Budget Surplus

Scenario:

Principal Alisha Pandey of Ellora Elementary School learned that the school has a 50L budget surplus due to lower-than-expected maintenance costs. The school board expects her to submit a proposal for using the funds by the end of the month. The school's ageing playground equipment needs replacement, but teachers have also requested additional classroom technology, such as tablets, to support individualized learning. Meanwhile, a parent group is lobbying for an after-school arts program.

Advice Given:

The business manager, Tanuja, advises Aisha to prioritize the playground, citing safety concerns and potential liability if they are not addressed. The instructional coach, Lalit Kapoor, argues for the tablets, noting that technology could boost student engagement and test scores, aligning with district goals. The PTA president, Malti Bajaj, suggests splitting the funds: 30L for the playground and 20L to pilot the arts program, arguing it's a compromise that addresses multiple needs.

Decision Point:

Aisha must decide how to allocate the funds—or whether to push for a larger budget next year to tackle all priorities. How should she justify her choice to stakeholders with competing interests?

Decision & Justification for Budget Allocation

After careful consideration of the school's needs, stakeholder priorities, and long-term benefits, Principal Aisha Pandey decides to allocate the ₹50 lakh surplus as follows:

₹30 lakh – Playground Renovation (Safety & Liability)

₹20 lakh – Pilot After-School Arts Program (Student Well-Being & Community Engagement)

Justification to Stakeholders:

1?? To the Business Manager, Tanuja:
"Student safety is non-negotiable. By prioritizing the playground renovation, we mitigate liability risks while ensuring students' safe and engaging outdoor space."

2?? To the Instructional Coach, Lalit Kapoor:
"While technology is valuable, investing in it immediately would serve only a portion of our students. We can explore alternative funding sources for classroom tablets next year, possibly through grants or district funding."

3?? To the PTA President, Malti Bajaj & Parents:
"The arts program enhances creativity and provides an inclusive opportunity for all students. Piloting it with ₹20L allows us to measure impact before expanding in the future."

4?? . To the School Board:
"This allocation balances urgent safety needs with student enrichment. However, we recognize the importance of technology and will advocate for additional funding next year to support classroom innovation."

By addressing immediate safety concerns while investing in creative development, this decision satisfies multiple stakeholders while ensuring a well-rounded approach to student growth. ?

#SchoolLeadership   #BudgetAllocation
#StudentSuccess #EducationMatters

69

CHAPTER FOUR

Research Findings: Leadership Skills For Heads of Schools

A great school leader is not just a decision-maker but an inspiration, guiding students and teachers toward excellence.

Collaboration and distributed leadership are key to effective school management. They promote shared responsibility and improve outcomes.

Research suggests that effective school managers are visionary, build trust, and focus on teaching and learning.

It seems likely that traits like communication, data-driven decisions, and community engagement are crucial.

The evidence leans toward distributed leadership and resilience, which are critical for school success.

Depending on the school context, there's some debate on how much instructional versus transformational leadership matters.

Effective school managers exhibit visionary, relational, and strategic traits, with distributed leadership and data-driven decisions having a particularly impactful impact.

Effective school managers are visionary, setting clear objectives and anticipating future challenges.

Leadership Traits and Strategies in School Management

CHAPTER FIVE

Top 25 Dos' & Don'ts For A School Principal

Dos (Things a Principal Should Do)

1.

   Lead by example – Demonstrate integrity, professionalism, and a strong work ethic.

2.

   Prioritize student safety – Implement clear policies and emergency preparedness.

3.

   Communicate effectively – Keep staff, students, and parents informed transparently.

4.

Support teachers – Provide resources, training, and encouragement.

5.

Listen actively – Value input from students, staff, and parents in decision-making.

6.

Set clear goals – Develop a vision with measurable outcomes.

7.

Foster inclusivity – Ensure all students feel valued and respected.

8.

Build relationships – Connect with students, staff, and families.

9.

Stay visible – Engage with school life by visiting classrooms and events.

10.

Encourage innovation – Support creative teaching methods.

11.

Manage resources wisely – Allocate budget and personnel effectively.

12.

Celebrate successes – Recognize student and staff achievements.

13.

Stay calm under pressure – Handle crises with composure.

14.

Promote a positive culture – Foster respect, teamwork, and enthusiasm.

15.

Keep learning – Stay updated on educational trends and leadership strategies.

16.

Delegate effectively – Trust staff with responsibilities to optimize workflow.

17.

Enforce discipline fairly – Apply rules consistently and with empathy.

18.

Collaborate with parents – Involve families in education as partners.

19.

Monitor student progress – Use data to adjust learning strategies.

20.

Advocate for your school – Seek district and community support.

21.

Maintain confidentiality – Protect sensitive student and staff information.

22.

Plan strategically – Develop long-term academic and operational goals.

23.

Embrace accountability – Take responsibility for school performance.

24.

Encourage teamwork – Promote staff collaboration for problem-solving.

25.

Show empathy – Address emotional and mental health needs.

? Don'ts (Things a Principal Should Avoid)

1.

Don't micromanage – Allow teachers autonomy in their classrooms.

2.

Don't ignore feedback – Value concerns from staff, students, and parents.

3.

Don't play favorites – Treat all students and staff equitably.

4.

Don't neglect self-care – Avoid burnout to stay effective.

5.

Don't avoid tough decisions – Address issues proactively.

6.

Don't lose sight of students – Administrative work shouldn't overshadow student needs.

7.

Don't tolerate bullying – Address harassment immediately and firmly.

8.

Don't overpromise – Be realistic about commitments.

9.

Don't isolate yourself – Be approachable and engaged.

10.

Don't resist change – Adapt to new educational methods.

11.

Don't disregard data – Use evidence to improve performance.

12.

Don't communicate poorly – Avoid vague or inconsistent messaging.

13.

Don't neglect teacher morale – Support and uplift your staff.

14.

Don't break promises – Keep commitments to build trust.

15.

Don't enforce rules blindly – Consider context before disciplinary action.

16.

Don't overlook mental health – Address student and staff well-being.

17.

Don't waste resources – Use time, money, and personnel efficiently.

18.

Don't dismiss parents – Collaborate instead of viewing them as adversaries.

19.

Don't shy away from conflict – Address issues before they escalate.

20.

Don't take credit unfairly – Acknowledge team contributions.

21.

Don't let politics dominate – Keep focus on student success.

22.

Don't neglect professional growth – Continuously improve leadership skills.

23.

Don't react impulsively – Make well-thought-out decisions.

24.

Don't ignore legal obligations – Ensure compliance with educational laws and policies.

25.

Don't forget your 'why' – Stay committed to making a meaningful impact in education.

CHAPTER SIX

TOP AI TOOLS FOR HEADS OF SCHOOLS

Google Classroom - Integrates AI to manage assignments, track student progress, and facilitate communication, reducing administrative workload.

Classcraft - Uses AI to gamify classroom management, helping heads monitor engagement and behavior trends across the school.

PowerSchool - An AI-enhanced student information system (SIS) for managing enrollment, grades, and attendance, offering analytics for school-wide insights.

Schoology - A learning management system (LMS) with AI features to streamline scheduling, assessments, and performance tracking.

Edmentum - Provides AI-driven personalized learning paths and data analytics to inform school-wide instructional strategies.

Century Tech - Uses AI to deliver adaptive learning and real-time analytics, helping heads identify areas needing intervention.

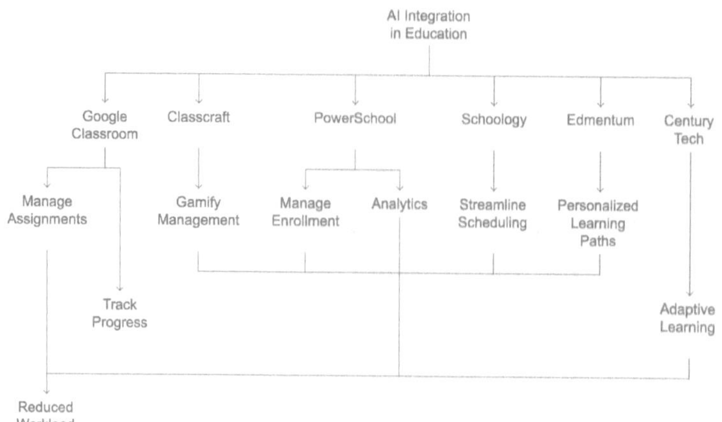

DreamBox Learning - An AI-powered math platform with reporting tools for heads to assess curriculum effectiveness.

Kaltura - An AI-enhanced video platform for managing valuable educational content for training staff and sharing school updates.

BrightBytes - Offers AI-driven data analytics to evaluate technology use, student outcomes, and school climate.

Allovue - An AI tool for financial management, helping heads optimize budgets and resource allocation.

Fetchy - A generative AI platform tailored for educators that assists with administrative tasks

like drafting policies or newsletters.

Gradescope - Automates grading with AI, providing heads with performance data to assess teaching efficacy.

AI Tools in Education Management

DreamBox Learning

An AI-powered math platform with reporting tools for assessing curriculum effectiveness.

Kaltura

An AI-enhanced video platform for managing educational content and sharing updates.

BrightBytes

Offers AI-driven data analytics to evaluate technology use, student outcomes, and school climate.

Allovue

An AI tool for financial management, optimizing budgets and resource allocation.

Fetchy

A generative AI platform for educators, assisting with administrative tasks like drafting policies or newsletters.

Gradescope

Automates grading with AI, providing performance data to assess teaching efficacy.

Khanmigo (Khan Academy) - An AI assistant for lesson planning and student tutoring, with analytics for school-wide progress tracking.

Magic School AI - Offers over 70 AI tools for lesson planning, assessments, and administrative support, ideal for school-wide implementation.

Eduaide.AI - An AI workspace for creating resources and analyzing student data, supporting heads in curriculum oversight.

Socrat - Enables heads to monitor class creation, assignments, and student engagement through AI-driven insights.

Carnegie Learning - Provides AI-based platforms (e.g., MATHia) with detailed reporting for academic performance management.

Brisk Teaching - An AI tool to streamline teacher workflows, giving heads visibility into instructional efficiency.

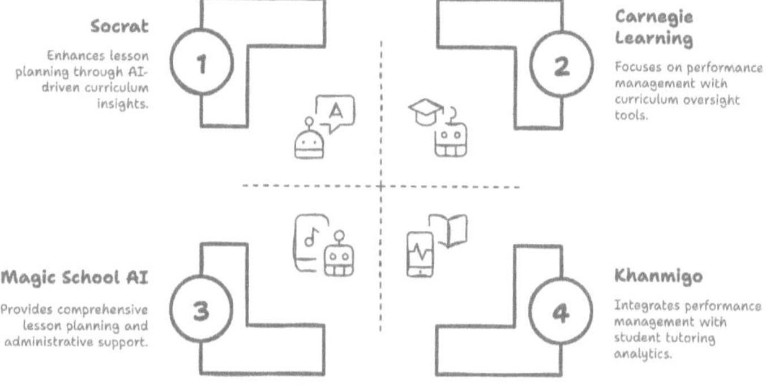

Quizizz - Uses AI to generate assessments and track engagement, offering school-wide data for heads to review.

Disco AI - An AI-powered LMS for managing professional development and branded academies that is useful for staff training.

Amira Learning - An AI literacy tool with diagnostics to help heads address reading gaps across grade levels.

Squirrel AI - Offers adaptive learning and analytics, enabling heads to tailor interventions for diverse learners.

Packback - An AI platform for online discussions, providing engagement metrics for school-wide evaluation.

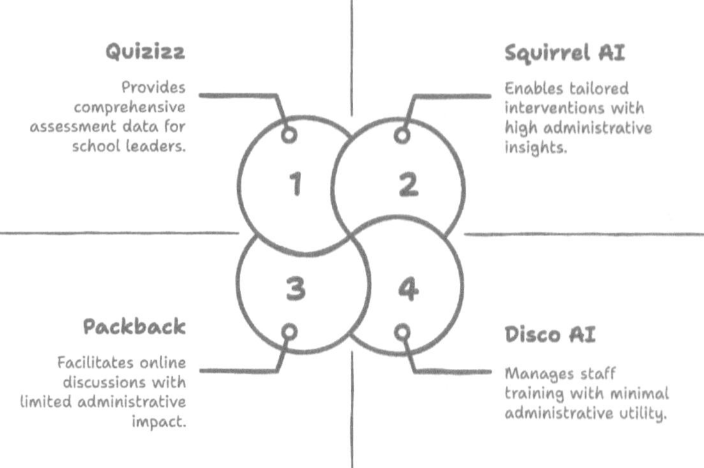

SafeStop - An AI-driven transportation management tool ensuring efficient bus routing and safety oversight.

Darktrace - An AI cybersecurity solution to protect school networks, critical for heads managing digital infrastructure.

Why Do These Tools Matter for Heads of Schools?

Heads of schools juggle multiple responsibilities—overseeing academics, managing staff, ensuring financial health, and maintaining a safe, effective learning environment. These tools leverage AI to automate repetitive tasks (e.g., grading and scheduling), provide actionable data (e.g., student performance and budget trends), and enhance decision-making (e.g., identifying at-risk students or optimizing resources). Tools like PowerSchool and BrightBytes offer high-level insights. In contrast, others like Magic School AI and Fetchy directly support teachers, freeing them to focus on instruction—a key concern for school leaders.

Books By The Same Author

About The Authors

Dr. Dheeraj Mehrotra is a distinguished educational leader and innovator with over three decades of experience transforming education through excellence and innovation. A recipient of the President of India's National Teacher Award (2006), he is a certified expert in Six Sigma (White and Yellow Belt), Neuro-Linguistic Programming (NLP), and Total Quality Management (TQM). His specialisation encompasses academic audits, school quality assurance and accreditation (SQAA), and implementing Kaizen and 5S in schools. As an accomplished author, Dr. Mehrotra has published over 200 books on various subjects, including computer science, artificial intelligence, digital body language, quality circles, and school management. His contributions also include the development of more than 150 free educational mobile apps for teachers, students, and parents, a feat recognised by the Limca Book of Records and the India Book of Records. Dr. Mehrotra has served as Principal at prestigious institutions such as De Indian Public School in New Delhi, NPS International School in Guwahati, and Kunwar's Global School in Lucknow. He has also held the position of Education Officer at GEMS in Gurgaon, making significant contributions to the global education community. As a premier UDEMY instructor, Dr. Mehrotra has created over 500 courses that have impacted more than 800,000 learners across 180 countries. Additionally, as the founder and president of the IoT Society of India, he advocates for technology integration in education worldwide.

Zeba Parveen is the Founder and Director of Zeba International Education of Scholarbirds (ZIES), an Uttar Pradesh-based organization established in January 2018. A visionary leader in the education sector, she is dedicated to promoting accessible and quality education by bridging the gap between national and international universities and students in India. Under her leadership, ZIES has played a pivotal role in facilitating institutional collaborations, organizing educational events, and enhancing learning opportunities. With a passion for academic excellence and innovation, Zeba Parveen continues to empower students and educators, shaping a brighter future for education in India.